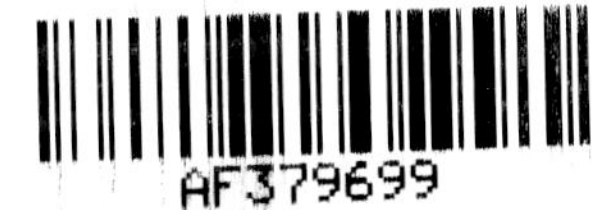

AF379699

table of contents

CPSIA information can be obtained
at www.ICGtesting.com
Printed in the USA
LVIC060111221019
634938LV00003B/185